Seasons
of the Soul

Seasons of the Soul

An Intimate God in Liturgical Time

Carla Mae Streeter, O.P.

New City Press
Hyde Park, New York

Published in the United States by New City Press
202 Comforter Blvd., Hyde Park, NY 12538
www.newcitypress.com
©2012 Carla Mae Streeter

Cover design by Durva Correia

Library of Congress Cataloging-in-Publication Data

Streeter, Carla Mae.
  Seasons of the soul : an intimate God in liturgical time / Carla Mae Streeter.
    p. cm.
  ISBN 978-1-56548-451-1 (pbk. : alk. paper) 1. Church year meditations. 2.
Catholic Church. I. Title.
  BX2170.C55S795 2012
  263'.9--dc23

                              2012017608

Printed in the United States of America

Contents

Nature
the Creator's loom
weaves
the Seasons of the Soul
thread by thread
revealing the pattern
of our journey home.

Jeanne Burg, O.P.
(Adapted)

Introduction

The Church Is a Woman-in-Love

*T*his introduction may seem a bit flippant at first glance. The church a woman-in-love? Holy *Mother* Church perhaps, or the *New Jerusalem,* but dare we use so erotic a reference in good taste? I suggest that we must not only dare, but are compelled to use this most passionate image as the very foundation of understanding the church as mother and as new Jerusalem. The words trip off our tongues, but what do the words *mean?*

We know well what being in love means. The condition grabs you and makes you weak in the knees. A magnetic force draws you to the beloved when he enters a room. You have the undignified urge to throw yourself into his arms in the midst of a room full of people. You go about your tasks a different person. You *are* a different person. Now you are in love, and before you weren't. You see differently. Why didn't I notice those birds before, those clouds before, those faces before? Why does the rain look different? Why do I feel as though I've been pierced, and my very soul is leaking out? Why am I so filled with joy? Why wouldn't I trade this for anything, and like a fool, I welcome the sweet pain it brings, the longing it creates in me?

Given time, the first flush of infatuation passes, its thin skin giving way to the tough hide of a faithful love, stronger than death and harder than hell. Self-less and self-sacrificing, mature love is so identified with the beloved that it no longer knows where the other ends and I begin. Oh I know it well enough physically, but I can't find the dividing line between our souls. It has blurred, and I find myself often in him and he in me, and I wouldn't want it any other way. I know through my loving what my beloved is thinking. His love knows how I feel before I reveal it.

The church is a community with a *magnificent obsession.* The movie by this name told the tale of a young playboy who frittered away his youth flitting from one pleasure to the next. In his disdain for others he drove his open-air convertible around recklessly. He hit a young girl and blinded her, so severe were her injuries. His friends looked for him in vain when he disappeared from the social scene. We next find him enrolled in medical school. He has one goal: to become a neurosurgeon, and to find that little girl and offer to operate to try to restore her sight. He finished his studies and became famous for his skill. He searched for and eventually found the little girl, now a grown woman, living in the blindness he had caused. She consents to the surgery, and he does restore her sight. Then he marries her. The story of his magnificent obsession reads like a fairytale come true.

I suggest the church has a magnificent obsession. She cannot take her mind off her Beloved. His life as it unfolds in the gospel is her obsession. She ponders each event, wonders at his decisions for her sake, and weeps as he is destroyed. He seeks her out in rising, and breathes his own breath into her to make her strong for her pilgrimage through time. Then he will return and claim her, with all her children. When she takes her gaze from him she risks the danger of becoming a whore, sinking in corruption and misuse of power. When she remains fixed on him she blossoms, becoming fruitful. Her children learn from her the gaze that makes mystics.

We delight in lovers, whether they be tragic as in *West Side Story,* or hilarious as in *My Big Fat Greek Wedding.* But what evidence do we have that the church is such a lover? The clearest piece of evidence is how the church handles time. Since before the calendar had been accepted with its three hundred and sixty-five day year, the church has used time to remember her Beloved. The seasons of nature set the stage for the seasons of the soul. Spring with its newness and beauty recalls the blush of her own discovery and exuberant joy. Summer celebrates her fruitfulness, and the rich variety of gifts in her household. Autumn with its muted beauty brings a harvest of ripe fruit, even as living things begin to fade away and sleep. Winter in its dull days and frozen beauty recalls the tomb, the waiting, and heaviness of death's sleep. Like the prelude to some magnificent fugue, nature announces the Paschal Mystery in its dying and rising. But the church is not a nature priestess honoring the Great Force. She is a woman in love with Someone. Her Beloved is not some mythic hero. He is more than the great Prince in search of his Cinderella. He is God's very Word married to her flesh, to her humanness, never to be parted. Her Christ has feet, and *they* walk in the dust. He has blood, and it will be poured out. He has arms, and they will be outstretched. He has a human heart and it will hang open. He has a mouth, and it will speak. He was born, he lived, and he died. He ate, slept, laughed, and cried.

The seasons of the soul are the seasons of the church's year. They are our seasons, for we collectively are the woman-in-love. Time itself with its seasons becomes a means of remembrance. The word *liturgy* means the people's work, worship-work of grateful love. The church's love prompts grateful remembrance. Her need to remember creates the liturgical seasons for what lies hidden in the ritual of the church. The church gathered celebrates in ritual what is unfolding in the cosmos, in the countryside, in the home, and in the heart. The woman-in-love remembers, and then begins remembering all over again. For hidden in her Jewish origins, the church has never lost the insight that as she remembers, she herself is created anew. What has happened in time has a meaning that endures, and ever-ancient, ever-new, she recognizes the mystery at work in her still, making her fruitful, and giving her children. The church continues to be born from this remembrance. The liturgical seasons are the fountainhead of her life. The liturgical seasons are the settings for the pearl that is the Word.

The first of these seasons is Advent, celebrated in the northern hemisphere in late fall, early winter. The season of longing, it captures the longing born of religious love that we call hope. The church enters once again into the longing of her own heart, which hollows her out once again to welcome the One who is always coming.

Introduction

Christmastide is the season of wonder, of surprise, the season of the Gift. It is also the season of the gradual return of light. Wide-eyed with wonder at the coming of her Beloved, garmented in the flesh that is her own, the church celebrates with wild yet reverent joy. It is the season of the gradual dawning of the knowledge that is born of religious love we call faith.

The joy of Christmastide gives way to the exposures, the discoveries, of the Epiphany season. That he has come is one thing. Who he is, is something else altogether. The season of manifestation, of revelation, Epiphany is the season of the lifting of the veil, the season of the icon, the window into the holy, right in our midst. The knowing born of religious love that is faith deepens as the heart opens in wonder.

Bolstered by wonders, we are equipped for the Lenten journey. Lent is the season of springtime. It is the season of melting, of turning over the soil of human hardness so the seed can sink in and grow. Lent is repentance time, the season of weeping and of mercy. It will be capped by the Triduum, the three special days of Holy Week: Holy Thursday, Good Friday, and Holy Saturday. It is the hard time of looking into the face of Love rejected, and knowing that I have done the rejecting.

The Easter season bursts upon the church like the fireworks of the Fourth of July. The resurrection is God's answer to death's stranglehold, to human violence and abuse, to despair and hopelessness. The Easter season is the season of promise, fifty days, ten beyond the forty days of Lent. This timing is not incidental. It is intentional. It is the church's honest and realistic salute to the agony of the passion. But it is also a tipping of the weight of the scales in the direction of resurrection victory, glory, and promise.

The Easter season ends with the feast of Pentecost, the coming of the Holy Spirit. What follows is a small space of time in which special feasts are celebrated. These feasts, that of the Trinity, Corpus Christi (or the Body of Christ), and the feasts of the heart of Christ and his mother-the Sacred Heart of Jesus and the Immaculate Heart of Mary-penetrate the consciousness of the church with keen insights. No mere pious devotionalism, these feasts have much to teach the church about itself. Is the mystery of the Three-in-One merely an ancient abstraction, fabricated by theologians who had time on their hands? Or is it the breakthrough about Divine Mystery the entire world has been waiting for? What does it mean to honor the *heart* of Christ and that of his mother? Is this some pious Catholic hangover? And what are we to make of the presence of Christ in bread? Mere remembrance, or actuality? What meaning could this possibly have for the modern man and woman? What insights about ourselves are hidden here, waiting to be uncovered?

With these feasts celebrated, the church enters into its longest season, the season of Ordinary Time. Truly a reflection of real life, this season uncovers the hidden mystery at work in the ordinary, the times of ordinary faithful Christian living. This is the time of summer and early fall, the time of fruitfulness and harvest. The celebrations of these weeks open up the treasures of the Word at work in the church's day-to-day life and struggles. It is the time of weaving, of integration. The threads of all the seasons are woven together each *year* with a new pattern, for we are different, and how we respond to our memories keeps changing us. The fabric of our lives reflects anew the dark tones of sorrow and loss and bright hues of birth, joy, and fruitfulness. It is the season of action born of religious love, the active love we call charity.

With her eyes on the One she loves, the church prepares to begin again, to return to Advent and its longing. Aware that she is made new again by the continual action of the Spirit, his final gift, she sets out again on her pilgrim journey, knowing she has not yet arrived, that she must still welcome him anew, wonder, discover, repent, be cleansed, and be healed. Foreshadowed in the transformation of the fairytale Cinderella, the transformation of this humble human maid is real. The end of this dance, the dance of the seasons of the soul, is no back-to-usual stroke of midnight curse. It is a dance for the rest of her life, moving deeper into unending union with her Prince.

I dedicate these reflections to the Sisters of Notre Dame, Milwaukee Province, in particular Carolyn Stahl, S.S.N.D., who taught me to love the liturgy as a child. I am grateful to Catherine Vancie, R.S.H.M., for her reading of the text and her insightful suggestions.

Carla Mae Streeter, O.P.

Cinderella

Busy anxious scrubber,
apron safe in place
to hide the threadbare
clothing of the heart
beneath.

Look up, broom-Lady,
see who bends before you
in the human grime
towel and basin ready.
He comes a-wooing with a gift
to laugh away the dirt and tears —
footwear for a journey
transparent — clear to see the loved earth by.

Homespun
well he knows.
A strong right arm lie offers for the dance.
Look up, broom-Lady.
See yourself —
reflected in his eyes.

C.M. Streeter, O.P., 1980

Advent:
the Season of Longing

The Key to Who I Am

Advent's color is midnight blue-purple. It is a time of darkness, of night. The night of this time is broken only by the tiny pinpoints of light the stars provide. "Long is our winter, dark is our night ... Oh come set us free, O saving light ..." goes the old song. The drama of the church's year begins with emptiness, with a void. Yet in that void there is something. There is an ache. The ache of the heart is a yearning, a longing, a hunger, a desire. We humans are a long-loving desire. We are a longing that is realizing itself. Perhaps that is what potentiality means. We are pure potential becoming increasingly real.

Human longing is a desire within a desire. Deepest of all there is the desire for that which is more — more than myself, more than what I can see, touch, taste, smell, hear, feel. It is a longing for Transcendence, for that which is Mystery, beyond my mind's grasp. Those that kill this longing in themselves are left with nothing but themselves. Perhaps that is a definition of hell — the human being forever confined to itself, locked within the prison of its limits, sealed up in a potential on perpetual hold, shriveled, drying up, and limp.

The religions of the world have different names for the Transcendent, or, like Buddhists, refuse to name it altogether, not because they are atheists, but because they refuse to squeeze the Transcendent into a human concept. The most common name for the Mystery is God, but one must be careful. The word *God* can mean only what the sayer wants it to mean. The word *God* can mean only what one's tradition will allow it to mean. But the Mystery laughs. The human does not define the Mystery. Rather, it is the Mystery that brings forth the human. The Mystery will not be confined to any wording, any definition, any description. All such attempts are but feeble efforts to confine the sea of Mystery to the thimble of the mind.

From history's earliest records, it is clear that humans have sought the Mystery, however they thought or spoke of it. The longing, the ache, the hunger for the Holy is there. But with it is terror. William James called it *facinans et tremendum:* fascination and terror. But why the fear? The Mystery is hidden, and its primary revelation is nature. The cosmos is the primary text of the Holy. Thunder, earthquake, tidal wave, fire, hurricane — all can dwarf the human into an insignificant whimper. Dew drop, spider web, sunrise, snowflake — these can scoop the human up in wide-eyed wonder. Is it any surprise, then, that animism, the worship of nature as divine, is the primal religious response? Yet with the birth of questioning came science, and with science came explanations for thunder, earthquake, sunrise, and snowflake. Alongside this discovery of the mind came the religious traditions of the East, the

Middle East, and the religions of the Book — Judaic, Christian, and Islamic. The experience of the Holy still plays in nature, but now moves in history. The law becomes a text in Torah. The human becomes a text in Jesus, and submission becomes the text of humans' response to the Holy in the Qur'an.

Core as it is, the ache for intimacy with the Holy is only part of the story. The human longs for intimacy with the human. There are those who say it is one unified longing for communion, the human manifestation of a dynamic that is manifested in the cosmos in a thousand ways: the allure of particles in physics, the gravitational lure of planets, the seduction of the peacock in full plumage, and the sexual attraction of man and woman. The ache of human sexual longing is all the more acute because it is self-reflexively conscious. We *know* we ache for human touch.

We tend to separate these two longings. Sexual longing couldn't possibly have anything to do with our hunger for God, could it? I propose that when the two dimensions of this longing are separated, promiscuity is the result. When they are kept unified, chaste love has a chance. Longing for human intimacy leans up against our longing for God and draws the strength to endure the asceticism of waiting. Our times are sex-obsessed, and spiritual hunger is widespread. The absence of a genuine intimacy with the Holy tempts us to plug the emptiness with the pacifier of sexual dalliance. Those who know they are empty of God know that only God can fill the emptiness. It is important to know how one is empty. Human intimacy can never still the longing only God can fill.

The ache of the human heart for God is called hope. It is longing born of religious love. As Christians we believe that we live always in hope. We live always in advent. Of ourselves we have no being. We draw being from the One who is. Christian conviction holds that I do not have any real existence apart from this relationship. Said simply, I live in God or I do not have real enduring life. I am "a dead man, a dead woman, walking." This conviction puts us in a position of radical poverty before God. I literally have nothing of my own. I draw my very being from this One who gives me life. Others have been instruments of that giving — my parents, my mentors, and all those who have helped me become who I am. But it also puts me in a position of radical wonder. For I am a most amazing being. I have a history and a story. I will be different tomorrow because of what happens today. I love wildly, and hope expectantly, and believe resolutely. I laugh and cry, dance and sing, and argue my convictions. This fact puts me in a most marvelous position to ponder Advent in its deepest significance.

My humanness flourishes because it is in relationship with that Holy, whether I acknowledge it or refuse to acknowledge it. When I acknowledge it, I come into a most amazing truth. *There is Someone in this dark with me.* (Thank you, Jessica Powers!) My Christian life is one of seeing in a glass darkly. But Someone is with me, or I couldn't even be. What would happen if I remembered this quietly each morning? What would happen if I remembered this often during the day? What would happen if I were assured of this fact in crisis?

This fact, that I am not alone, even if I forget and think I am, is revealed to us in the most concrete of ways: a woman carrying a child in her womb. With this image, the church begins its remembrance of its own reality. It is carrying life, and it is being carried. With this Advent remembrance we rediscover the place of the Mother of God.

Note well: Mary is a humble peasant girl of the Galilee region. Galilee was a mosquito-infested swamp area. Nobody who was anybody was from Galilee. The messenger of God comes to this young girl and announces that God wants to take on humanness from her. Would she be willing to give God a body? Young she may be, but she is intelligent enough to ask a question. She finds out what she needs to know. How is this to happen when I'm not sexually active? The messenger of God replies that God will supply for this usual activity. With an amazing sense that her being indeed draws its existence from the Divine, she says she will of course be part of the divine plan. And lo, as the nine months unfold, she is indeed with child, through the power of the Holy Spirit, the gospel says without blinking. Modern skeptics dismiss the virgin birth as incredible. It may be more intelligent to admit such skepticism lacks imaginative possibility.

Mary is me. She is you, and you, and you. Mary is that humanness that is asked to bring forth God. Evidence. She is to do this virginally, not because God doesn't like sex, but because what is being said here is beyond its capability. A man can't have a baby. But men are to birth God in the world as well as women. It is beyond sexuality. Sexuality is its herald.

Sexuality is its sign. But the herald is not the message.
The herald is servant of the message. The message
of God united with humanness in a woman's womb
is the message that for me, too, locked in the darkness of faith's womb in this life, this Holy One is
still taking on humanness: *mine*. Mary is a mirror.
In her we find our own original face as God-bearer.

This realization can stun us to silence. So we sit
in Advent darkness pondering who is with us in the
dark. Mary must have sat often, heavy with the life
in her womb, wondering what on earth was happening. How could this be, that the Holy One was
weaving flesh for Himself from her body and from
her faith? We join her in her pondering. How can
it be that the Holy One is not content with one full
human manifestation in history, but has arranged
mystically to be revealed again and again through
the likes of me? And by a continual virgin birth, if
you please, how else? Mary's role is not only a mirror
for me personally, it is a mirror for all of us com-
munally. The church's role in the world is to bring
forth the Christ. This is the church's mission. The
woman of the book of Revelation is bringing forth
the child the dragon wants to devour. The woman is
the church. The woman is us. Mary in her mother-
hood of the Word of God in the flesh is the sign of
the life carried by the woman-in-love, the church.

What will this child, born of us, born of the church,
look like? He will look like me. How will we know
there has been a birth? What is the evidence? My
decisions will tell the tale. There is precious little in
the gospels about Mary, and what is there is usually
avoided because to take it seriously we would have

to face our role in the world more seriously than we have done as a Christian community in the past. The Magnificat of Luke 1:46-55 is downright embarrassing when we read these words as the proclamation of the church. But these words are to be the church's manifesto in the world. If they truly were, we would not be able to do business as usual.

> *My soul magnifies the Lord,*
> *and my spirit rejoices in God my Savior,*

These words are attesting to a key relationship. I am in relationship with my God. In that right relationship I am filled with joy. Can I say this as an individual? What if the church said it? What would the world see? What witness would this give?

> *for he has looked with favor on*
> *the lowliness of his servant.*

What kind of self-concept is here? There is clearly a keen awareness of proportion. I am but a creature. The Holy One looks with favor on my littleness. Can I dare to look with favor on my littleness, or am I convinced I've got to make myself big? What does it mean to have a swollen soul? One that is puffed up? Is it all right to be little? Rather than size, does it mean owning my vulnerability? If I'm a servant then I'm not in charge. How then will I exercise power? How will the church then exercise power? How would it present itself? What witness would it give?

> *Surely, from now on all generations will call me blessed;*

Me, blessed? Holy? And everyone agreeing it's true? What would happen if I lived my humdrum life as though it was really blessed? What would happen to my attitude? And yet, is this not just what my baptism has done to me? Made me blessed? How would this remembrance change what I choose to do? Can we honestly say our church is called blessed by all the generations past and present? The church has to deal with concrete things: people's needs, structure, beliefs, worship. And Mary, too, dealt with very concrete things: the needs of her family, housing, her Jewish religion. What witness would blessedness bring to the world?

> *for the Mighty One has done great things for me,*
> *and holy is his name.*

Aha! Back to the relationship from line one. Because of this relationship, because I'm not in charge, the One who is Mighty is able to do great things for and through me. There is no swollenness of soul here. There is simple truth flowing from a relationship. Some great things have happened, and to me. God has done this in me. And by the way, his name is *holy*. I am in relationship to one who is very holy. What would happen if these became my words? The words of the church? What witness would this attitude have in the world?

> *His mercy is for those who fear him*
> *from generation to generation.*

Mercy is the overlooking of anything that might have offended through generous love. In the mouth of Mary these words are saying that those who know they are little and vulnerable before God, and even downright sinful, can expect to be wrapped in God's mercy. It is those who cover up these conditions, who pretend otherwise, who will be found uncovered. What would reflection on God's mercy do to my attitude toward others? What would it do in the church regarding those the church excludes?

> *He has shown strength with his arm;*
> *he has scattered the proud in the thoughts of their hearts.*

We all know what it is to feel the hard muscles of a strong man's arm. We know the security of leaning on someone's strong arm. We also know the arrogance of those who respect no one and nothing. Power is influence. I have power. There are certain people who are going to be influenced by me. How do I use my influence? When does my arrogance show? How does the church use its influence in the lives of its people? When does its arrogance show? What witness does this give in the world?

> *He has brought down the powerful from their thrones,*
> *and lifted up the lowly;*

What throne do I sit on? Has God had to bring me down a peg or two? What little one have I lifted up lately? Have I even noticed how others struggle? What throne does the church claim? Will God tolerate this? How does the church regard the lowliest of the lowly? Are we more concerned with paving the parking lot than with helping another have food to live? What witness does this give to the world?

> *He has filled the hungry with good things,*
> *and sent the rich away empty.*

Am I too full? Of what? Have I ever been really spiritually hungry? Have I admitted it? What does it mean to be rich? Does it mean my wealth is sterile? Petrified? It doesn't flow and give life? Is it like a spiritual hardening of the arteries? What does it mean for the church to be rich? What do we do with our resources? What witness does this give in the world?

He has helped his servant Israel,
in remembrance of his mercy,

Helping and mercy follow upon knowing the truth of my neediness. The mercy again is recalled as the overflowing compassion of love. How do I remember mercy? How does the church remember it? What is the church's witness of mercy in the world?

according to the promise he made to our ancestors,
to Abraham and to his descendants forever.

This line simply says that God will be faithful, that God will deliver. I am a descendant of Abraham. So are my Jewish and Islamic friends. The promise God made is that we would be able to live together in peace. What part do I play in bringing about that promise? How do I obstruct it? How does my church foster it? Obstruct it? What witness does this give to the world?

Spending time in Advent with the Mother of God is dangerous. It could have a transforming effect on my personal life and the life of the church. It is not by chance that Mary is on our minds during this season of the soul. She teaches us to keep watch and whistle in the dark. She teaches us to believe there is a new life within. She shows us how to hope. She models how to wait it out.

Flute

Cylinder
waiting-reed
poised for breath
and longing
silent ...

Sing
and tremble
as he passes.
At his touch
rejoice.

C.M. Streeter, O.P., 1982

Christmastide: the Season of Wonder

A Most Amazing Thing

The colors of this holiday season are green and red, but liturgically, this is a season of white-gold. The liturgical colors bespeak light. The season has everything to do with natural light. Although the understanding of solstice came later, the fact that daylight grew sparse in December was recognized in the ancient world. By December 25 it was clear that the days were getting longer, and so festivities were held. The Christians simply made this natural phenomenon the basis for celebrating the birth of the Christ, not knowing the real date, and not even having the Gregorian calendar yet at the time. They merely added Christian significance to festivities already in progress. The dark expectancy of the Advent season now gives way to the coming of the light. The lengthening of daylight was caused by the strengthening of the sun's stay in the daylight sky. The Christians focused on another Son, another Light that had entered the world.

The ancient religious traditions of the Far East were already part of the lives of millions of people. Thousands more paid tribute to the religion of Greece with its pantheon of gods and goddesses, and the religion of Rome with its divine emperors. India had its reincarnations and avatars revered by faithful devotees. What is interesting in these ancient traditions is the explicit awareness of a movement recently identified in our own day as a cosmic phenomenon: the movement toward *communion*. Described as an allurement, this cosmic thrust was acknowledged by these ancient wisdom traditions in various ways. While reverenced as totally *other,* at the same time the divine was presented as drawn to involvement with the human. So, while distinctive, the Christian mystery of the Incarnation was not an oddity or aberration at the time of the birth of Christianity. What was distinctive was the fact that Christianity had its origins in the Jewish tradition, and to image God in any way was blasphemous.

Rooted in the Torah, Jews and Christians believe that the human being was created in the image of God. The ancient Genesis text recounts this creation and depicts the human and divine relationship in terms of walking in the garden together as friends do, who have a bond between them. In the separation of the two traditions, Christians developed an understanding of sin as a rejection of the divine image. This is depicted in the expulsion from the garden, and the humans hiding from the God who comes to companion them. The broken image is presented to us as a loss of innocence, an ashamed awareness of nakedness. Eve is drawn from Adam's side in a type of gender-reversed virgin birth, and Eve draws Adam from trust in the Word of God to the isolation of a shattered friendship. This is the rich symbolic story of the reason for human darkness and the ever-present hunger for restored intimacy with the Holy. What then is the Christian answer to our Advent condition?

The answer is a wooing, a courtship, and a marriage. The bond was broken in a garden of delight. The bond will be restored in a garden of delight. The Song of Solomon (Song of Songs) recounts this wooing in explicit sexual terms. It is a book of the First Testament that has caused outright embarrassment to some. It portrays the Lover in hot pursuit of the beloved and their tryst in a garden.

The womb of the virgin is the new garden. The Christian scriptures present us with a reversal of the account of the loss. A woman, Mary, the new Eve, brings forth the new Adam in a virgin birth. The new Adam takes on the loss, the nakedness, by an amazing reversal: You have rejected my image in yourselves; I will therefore take on *your* image in myself. A most amazing thing.

The Incarnation of the Word of God in human flesh is in itself our redemption begun. As we will see, it is the beginning of the passion. The Incarnation is an indissoluble marriage: for better or for worse. The wedding chamber is the garden of Mary's person, her womb. From her DNA will be woven the image the Divine is assuming, and no part of the created universe will ever be the same. The attendants at the wedding are the very elements of the periodic table, and they tremble with joy at the honor. The body of the Word is woven of stardust, as is our own from one of our own.

The restoring of a lost image: It was not enough that the Word of God should shape the galaxies. It was not enough that it carve out the Law from

Sinai's stone. Nor was it sufficient that it permeate the consciousness of the prophet until the words burned to be released. It was not enough that the Spirit groans in the Vedas, and sighs in the breathing of bodhisattvas. Nor is it enough that writings and law prompt the total submission of the human heart to the Holy. It will be enough, it will be complete, only when the Spirit writes that Word again in the very image that rejected it, the human image. The image must be restored with flesh and blood. It is the Spirit, poised and breathless, who awaits a yes from the new Eve to begin the reversal. In the garden-body of Mary, the Spirit fuses together what a decision had torn asunder. The wedding contract is written on the very flesh of God. By the touch of God the image is restored. The human is joined to the Holy, never again to be parted.

The scriptural readings of Advent have prepared us, offering the ancient texts for our reflection again and again. A messenger comes to announce the plan to one considered *useless*. The virgin was unproductive, a waste, useless in terms of the Jewish tradition. Mary's virginity is a theological statement of our human condition. We are sterile, useless, unproductive. Nothing can come from us. The divine image in us is not destroyed, but broken and barren. Over this chaos, as in the beginning, the Spirit hovers. The humble Mary, the new earth, the new garden, says her yes to the plan, and gives God a body woven from her own humanness, her very own substance. Starting from the beginning that every mother knows, a human life gestates, fused to the Word of God. Silent, and speaking only in the hum of protoplasm, heartbeat, and fetal breathing, the Word dwells in the dark security of his mother's womb. No stage of the human is to be excluded from the plan. From the beginning all is to be assumed and all is to be restored.

What is being told to us by the marvel of this revelation? Even prior to the birth every element of the created world is invited to be part of the vesture of God. The positive view of creation, so soundly trumpeted in the First Testament, reaches symphonic proportions in the Incarnation. The silent music is wild with delight. The Psalms spoke of rivers clapping their hands and hills leaping like lambs. Here we have neurons and bone marrow, blood vessels and plasma, being knit together by the Spirit through the laws of nature in a cadence like some impassioned love theme.

The texts of Christmastide spin a story deceptively simple. Mary is found to be with child, and Joseph, her fiancé, knows he is not the father. Not understanding, he decides to divorce her quietly, for to do so publicly would result in her being stoned to death by Jewish law. In a dream he is told to take her as his wife, for the child she carries is God's doing. He does exactly as he is told, and we are left to wonder about the conversations between Mary and Joseph about all that had happened. Being from David's lineage, the couple goes to Bethlehem, David's city, because the text describes a census was being taken by the Romans, an occupying power. There is no room for them in the place for travelers, so the owner offers them shelter among the animals. In all probability this stable or animal shelter was underneath the house, the animals' bodies providing welcome heat for the residents above them. Here, in this shelter, the child Mary is carrying is born. We are not told who was there, or how the birth took place. We are told only that she wrapped the child in swaddling bands from head to foot. Out on the hillside the skies are filled with angels who announce the birth to shepherds tending their sheep. They come to find the child wrapped in the swaddling clothes, just as it was told them. Only two out of the four gospels report some of these events. What are we really being told?

The writing is happening after many years, and probably in the face of persecution of the early Christian community, so we must be careful about assuming historical detail. But we need make no mistake: We are being told much more than mere historical facts. We are being told about a mystery that the writer is convinced is not over. It is still working in the community. What is still working and how? And what difference might this make to our Christmas celebrations?

The mystery has been hidden. It has involved Mary and Joseph, and they have had to deal with it. The mystery is now becoming public. The secret is out. This is exactly what was happening to the early community. They had heard the preaching of the apostles, and the faith was spreading. Becoming public was putting many of them on the spot. Some of them were being driven from the synagogues because of their identification as Christians.

There is no place for the child. He doesn't fit. He's an intrusion. A count is being taken. The odd thing is that there is no record of this census. Those who are counted belong. Mary and Joseph go to be counted. They want to belong with the others. But they are rejected and housed with the animals. They are given the status of being "other," not with us. Was this a way of saying exactly what was happening to the community at the writing of the gospels?

Those in town and residing nearby have no idea of the birth. They are living their lives unaware. They are so close to it, but are blind to what is happening right in their midst. The poorest of the poor, those who take care of sheep and goats, the shepherds, are told what is going on. They are told by angels. Angels are messengers from God. What is the writer saying? That those who think they know really don't get it? That it takes a humbleness, an unpretentiousness, to get the message? That one must believe that others can be messengers from God for us? That the message comes in the night of our faith while we are tending to our ordinary business? The amazing thing is that the shepherds, these humble folks, believe the messengers. They go to find the newly born. They go to places where others would not go, to places where animals are kept.

They find the mystery child wrapped in swaddling clothes. Like a little mummy. Prepared ahead of time for burial. All wrapped up. Unable to move. Laid in a food trough. Bethlehem means "house of bread." Was the sacred writer saying that the child would be found in our own limitations? In our needing to keep a low profile? Was the gospel comforting Christians who needed to know the passion begins now? That we shouldn't be surprised we are rejected as he was, and condemned to die? That he feeds us with his very self when we gather as he told us? The shepherds understand. They know who they are, and because they do, they find the mystery hidden in the oddest unexpected place.

Are we really any different from those early folks? In the hustle and bustle of the holiday season will we notice what is essential, or will we miss the angels because we don't believe in visions in the night of our faith? Will we know where to look for the child? What are our unexpected places? Where is he being born today? Where are the "others"- the rejects, the ones excluded, the ones who impose, who don't fit? Will I miss him if he comes knocking? Will I be able to spot him in the midst of my ordinary business, in the darkness of my faith, when there are no spiritual lights on - only pinpointed stars now and then?

Why is he all wrapped up? Am I his wrappings? Is he bound by me, with me, in me? Is he with me in this mess, in this struggle I call my life? How come he makes himself so small? Is this a way to be God? This is a far cry from the Word of God on Sinai! He cries from hunger. Will he try to eat me if I pick him up, as babies do? What does he want? To hold onto my finger? To grasp my soul? He can't even talk. Afraid? Why would I be afraid of a baby! And perhaps that's just the point. Who indeed would be afraid of a baby ... and as writer Tad Dunne once asked in his art, who is wrapping who around one's little finger?

The wonder of this season of the soul is the wonder of a new revelation of God. The God Christians have come to know in Christ Jesus is another aspect of the God of Sinai. This same God is hungry to be held, to nurse, to eat human things. The God who made the mountain shake now sleeps in a woman's arms. This is the God of the still soft whisper, like a child breathing in its sleep. This is what this God wants to reveal. This is mercy to the point of accommodation; compassion to the point of self-emptying; love to the point of passion.

The message mustn't be lost on us. We are being told how much we are worth. We are also being told how precious every created reality is. This is worth pondering in a season when nature is asleep, locked in ice in certain places, and covered with a blanket of snow. But the hope of Advent waits expectantly, and with the coming of the Light our faith knows something will come from all this deadness. It seems so ridiculous. These trees will have leaves? Why, they are dead, don't you see? Flowers? The ground is lifeless and hard, frozen and bare. Yet even though we do not see, we know. This season teaches us to believe. With the coming of the little child the seed is in the world. The Light has come and the darkness will not overcome it, for the marriage has taken place, the bridegroom is here. Our humanness, no matter how perverse, will never be the same.

There is another angle of this season that shouldn't be missed. The coming of the Light into our darkness happens in *a family*. The Redeemer is no Lone Ranger. The relational and communal setting for this event is deliberate. First, Mary's relationship with Joseph needs to be straightened out, and it is, by divine intervention through-of all things-a dream. The Hebrew Scriptures are not shy in relating the interventions of angels. Yet here in this event, there is no special appearance as with the announcement to Mary. Instead, Mary is left to trust God will be faithful in working it out, and Joseph is attentive to his dreams. Both responses issue a call to us in the ordinariness of our lives.

Then comes the census. Unless we take note, we might miss the fact that Mary decides she must accompany Joseph as he tries to obey the demand, even at great inconvenience to herself in her condition. Whatever the historical facts are here, the relational message is unmistakable. The two have so bonded as a couple that in thick or thin they will face things together. It is the relational common life that forms the arms of welcome for the Light. This careful provision of a loving relational setting speaks volumes to us today in our age of instant marriage and no-fault divorce. The web of relationships needed to nurture a child is gently spread out before us as a part of this most amazing thing. For better or worse, the Holy One has thrown his lot in with the complexity of our family lives. They are no afterthought. They are part of the wonder.

Christmas Agnus Dei

Shepherd,
your shoulders bear the wood from birth
and stupefied sheep stand agape
in wonder.

Crag-like fingers wait your lifting
and the sun prepares to hide in shame.

From whence comes your robe
of homespun flesh, Shepherd?

"From a maid who wove it
on a loom of love," said he.
"From a maid who knows the pattern well
and can teach thee."

C.M. Streeter, O.P., 1982

Epiphany:
the Season of Exposure

God Plays Peek-a-boo

*T*his season of the soul is really still a part of Christmastide, but has a texture all its own. It shares the white-gold brilliance of the color spectrum, but as early winter wheat sprouts early, the dazzling white of this season gives way to the green of just a few weeks of Ordinary Time before Lent makes its appearance. The heart of the remembrance for the woman-in-love during this time is the ever-widening radiance of the Light. It is a time of widening exposure, a time of manifestation, a time of discovery.

Beginning in the darkness of an animal shelter, in the context of earthiness complete with the smells of bodily functions and the hot breath of beasts, the Light shows itself first to Mary and Joseph personally. Hidden for nine months in the depths of Mary's womb, the Light reveals itself first to Mary in the attentiveness she gives to the life she carries, and known only to her in its subtle movements. Joseph enters the widening circle by his simple faith in what he is told. With the birth, the Light reveals itself in the intimate communion of their committed love, expanding their love into a familial community. We mustn't miss being amazed at the flowering of selflessness that had to grow from this deeply earthy, personal, and relational beginning. We can't risk losing the implications this has for our own ongoing transformation and that of the Church. Everything begins in the unconditional surrender that is faith. The growth begins in the weaving of something from the fiber and tissue of our own frail humanness, and emerges perfectly at home in the humblest of surroundings.

The circumference widens next to include the shepherds. They come, they see, and they understand. The exposure has become public. The first to be included, thus setting an unmistakable priority, are those of no account. Shepherds. Peasants. Those who take care of animals. Make no mistake: The place was surrounded with folks with far better credentials, far better means, more noteworthy status. Yet the Light deliberately drew these simple ones first. Written between the lines of the gospel account is the clear message of God's priorities, and this preference clashes radically with how we often value people, both personally and as a Church.

But there is no lopsidedness here, leaving those of us who have means, education, and status out in the cold. The circumference of the Light again expands, drawing in not only the wealthy, the educated, the noble, but the other, *those not like us*. Only Matthew gives us an account of the visit of the Magi, and much ink has been spilled in trying to establish the historicity of this visit by scientifically identifying heavenly bodies that could have been the star that led the strangers to the child. Interesting as this might be, it can be a distraction, causing us to miss the point. The point is that the wealthy come, and offer their wealth. It is not frozen; it flows. These wealthy ones are educated, and they bring their education and do homage. Magi were the scientists of their day, learned ones who studied nature and the cosmos. Because of their wealth and education they have status. They bring their prestige and offer that.

But more than all this they come as non-Jews; they are not people of the Mosaic covenant. They may not even be people of the Abrahamic covenant. They are people of the Noetic covenant. They seek for the Holy in ways foreign to the tradition of this family, of the land they have entered as guests, and are left only with the humanity they share with the little child. This is the bridge — the common humanness. The Holy has spoken a word enfleshed that is common language. No manner of religious dogma, ritual practice, or moral injunction is considered here. Their ancient Eastern wisdom has told them of a special birth, and clothed in the richness of their ancient traditions, they come to pay honor. There is nothing here about them being converted. In fact, as the story unfolds, the child's tradition tries to deceive them. Herod lies to them. As with Joseph, it is a dream that guides them away from the trap. They listen to dreams, and so return safely to their own countries. They return. They do not stay where the newly found child is. But led by what they know, a sign in the heavens, these foreigners are the second "public" to find the Light.

As the Church ponders this particular Epiphany exposure, it is clear that the early Church was confronted with the question of pluralism, with those who are neither Jewish nor Christian, and their relation with the Light come into the world. Doctrinally this will become the question of salvation. It is clear that Christian identity calls for an explicit faith commitment to the person of Christ Jesus in his historical Jewish life, death, and resurrection. What is not clear is how we struggle to address the activity of the Word in the world through the Spirit *before, during,* and *after* the fullness of revelation received in Christ Jesus. The gospel account of the visit of the Magi opens this question to the Church for its consideration. What was the light that led them in their quest? What enabled them to find the child? What safeguarded their return to their way of life and thus affirmed the value of their lives? What is happening to them and how is it happening, when we find fullness in the explicit revelation of the Word of God in Christ Jesus?

The gifts they present to the child further complicate the pluralist issue. They offer him gold. The regal metal, gold is offered to monarchs, to royalty. These strangers seem to be acknowledging that there just may be One worth worshiping outside of the gods they know. Perhaps gold is the gift of all honest agnostics, those among us with the integrity to admit there is so much they really do not know.

They offer frankincense. In contrast to gold, which immediately delights the eye with its beauty, incense needs to be burnt before it releases the fullness of its aroma. Saturated with the sweet-smelling resin of trees, incense when it burns delights the sense of smell. Rather than a decor that enhances the beauty of the human through sight, this gift lifts the human above all that is seen into a realm beyond the senses.

The smell of incense is ecstatic; it draws us out of ourselves. It is a summons to attend to what is beyond the senses, and is used in all mainline religious traditions to captivate the human and direct attention to the Divine. Incense is often used as a symbol of prayer. Was this gift offered to suggest that the child needed to pray, or that the child was worthy of prayer? The ambiguity captures us and holds us; there is no release; there is no answer to the question. Perhaps it is the mission of Christians in the world to explain who the child is and thus answer the question.

Myrrh is the final gift. Perfumed burial ointment. Matthew could have easily borrowed the first two gifts from other references in the Hebrew Scriptures. But this third gift is missing from those texts. It is this gift that supports the conviction that this visit is a powerful midrash of the early Church as it begins to spread. Myrrh would not be brought ordinarily as a gift when visiting a new baby. Myrrh gives away the fact that the writer knows what eventually happens to the baby. The child will grow, and become a sign of contradiction. The child who has grown will suffer and die, and need to be buried. *And even in this dying there will be something beautiful, something ecstatic, something that lifts you out of yourself to the Divine.* There will be something special about this dying. There is a mystery in this dying, and so that is why this is a worthy gift for a special child. The simple account tells us no more. We are left with wonder provided by strangers; the *others.*

The dynamic of exposure, of discovery in this season, is not finished. The simple, the learned, the wealthy, the noble have been exposed to the Light.

A major group remains. The Light must be publicly exposed to the Jewish people to whom it has come, and in particular to those Jews who will be missioned to spread it: the apostles. The feast of the Baptism of Jesus by John the Baptist officially ends the Christmas/Epiphany season, and the account of the wedding at Cana completes the theme of exposure.

The person of John the Baptizer appeared during the Advent season. His role there was herald, pointing to the One who would come. It is John who kindles hope in our hearts, who stirs up longing in the darkness of our waiting. Salvation comes from the Jews. In the Epiphany season John has another role: He identifies the Light already in our midst. Jesus is in the crowd and steps forward to be baptized. John points and says, "Behold the Lamb of God ..." The exposure has reached out to the crowd, and it is this exposure of the Light that will set in motion the effort to snuff it out.

The Light is exposed for all to see. John objects. I should be baptized by you, he says to Jesus. But no, first of many brothers and sisters, Jesus enters the waters, and the waters of the earth are blessed evermore for that cleansing wash that will identify the Christian. Water, the blood substitute. Water, which will gush from a pierced side, an unending stream of mercy. The Light is in the water, consecrating it all over the earth. The sky opens, and John's identification is confirmed by heaven itself: "This is my beloved Son, hear him." And the Spirit, dove of fire, drives him into the desert to prepare him to be fixed on a pole to heal all who will look.

John directs the apostles to Jesus. They come and see, and then leave all to follow. John the evangelist alone presents us with an event where the disciples and the master are together for the first time. There is a wedding in Cana of Galilee, and Jesus and his disciples are invited. Mary is present, and she seems to have some authority among the servants. The wine runs out — not surprising considering that the wedding is in Galilee, one of the poorest sections of the Israel of that day. Mary goes to her son and tells him of the dilemma. He seems unconcerned. She directs the servants to do whatever he tells them. Jesus directs the servants to fill several large jugs with water. Then he tells a servant to take the contents to the chief steward to taste. The steward, unaware of what has happened, tastes, and remarks that the best wine has been saved until now. The story ends with the simple comment that this was the first of the signs Jesus worked, and his disciples believed in him.

The remarkable thing about these ever-widening circles of exposure is that in this final event, we come full circle back to where we started. It all began with a revelation of the Light to a select few, and now it returns to the select few: the apostles who are now to keep the circumference of the Light ever widening by their mission to the world.

The setting is a wedding. The setting is deliberate. Whether or not the wedding at Cana was ever a historical event, the setting is deliberate. There is to be a new union. The Divine is in hot pursuit of the beloved estranged human, and will not rest until the new creation begins. Again the Spirit hovers over the waters, and again the Word speaks. The insipid water of law alone is transformed by the very presence of the Bridegroom. At his approach the water blushes, and the humor in the story reaches a peak when the steward goes to the young bridegroom and says that the best wine has been saved until now. *The steward has gone to the wrong bridegroom.* The real Bridegroom stands there, having signed, in the water transformed into wine, the new union he has effected in his own person. The new creation has begun. He is the new creation. His disciples believe in him and we are invited to do the same.

The season of Epiphany closes, and for several weeks the Church goes into default mode: Ordinary Time. The community is still wide-eyed, as if captivated by a sunrise. It is a time of enchantment. The Light has come. It's wonderful. Like some magnificent symphony, the first major movement comes to a close, and a quiet transition prepares us for a somber second movement. With it, enchantment gives way to healthy disenchantment. Lent is on the horizon.

From Pad to Pad ...

We perch on his Rock
Waif-like
Eyes open wide
To catch a glimpse of Him
Hidden among the reeds.

Hearts in our throats
We open wide
To be fed
And to trumpet truth
With varied voices.

Hidden inside each
is a Prince.
Release Him
With a Holy Kiss!

C. M. Streeter, O.P., 1979

Lent:
the Season of Springtime

A Housecleaning of the Soul

*L*ent dons the richness of royal purple. Lent is the season of the reality check. What happens in this season of the soul is aptly imaged by a thorough spring cleaning. Once the light returns and the ice melts, the crisp air invites the womp of a carpet being shaken out. The accumulated winter grime on windows begs washing, and the crocus appears. Nature begins to stir, like some sleeper taking a stretch. Spring can't come fast enough it seems. Slowly the sap begins to run, but the trees still look like they will be dead forever.

In a frenzy of escape from self-restraint, Mardi Gras offers a last fling before Ash Wednesday for those who take Lent seriously. For those who don't take Lent seriously, these days of frolic simply offer a frenzy of escape from self-restraint. Deep within the human heart, covered over by layers of denial, there is an awareness of accountability. I am accountable to someone for my life. For some, it may be that I'm accountable to myself, or to someone I love. For the Church, the woman-in-love, the woman with the magnificent obsession, she is accountable to the One who loves her. His eyes become the mirror in which she sees herself as she really is.

As a reality check, Lent is a season to remember the facts. There is the fact that apart from this Holy One I have no existence. My body has been drawn from the elements of the earth through the love of my parents, and so this Holy One has determined that I shall be. I am made from Love and from dust, and to Love and to dust shall I return. This first fact is recalled by literally imprinting dust on the forehead on Ash Wednesday in the form of a cross. Made from the burnt palms of last year's victorious Palm Sunday, the blessed ashes are worn all that day, until washed away with the day's grime. With the ashes the revelry of Mardi Gras falls silent.

It is a critical moment. Unless the woman-in-love looks into the eyes of her Beloved at this point, there is danger of Lent becoming a self-flagellation, a wallowing in her shortcomings and her downright sins. It becomes a contest to see who can "give up" the most. Lent is not about giving up. It is about finding. It is about healing. It is about cleansing. It is about weeping. It is about reconciling. There will be no motivation for any of this if the lady is not in love. In the eyes of the Beloved she sees what she is looking for, what needs to be healed, what needs to be cleansed and reconciled, and she can weep with hope.

There are different kinds of tears. One can weep from grief or from loss. One can weep for joy and gratitude. Key to the weeping is the fact that something is very precious, something so dear that one is moved to tears when one thinks of it. It is quite a revelation to realize *why* one is weeping.

With her eyes not on herself, but on him and herself in him, the lady begins the forty days of Lent. Even the number of days recalls his time in the desert. Arbitrary though it is, the number indicates communion with him. So important is this communion, that whatever happens to him will also be happening to her. Only by maintaining this communion will she be able to face the fact that she is often the cause of what is happening to him. He has made it clear to her that he has taken on her humanness, for better or for worse. In doing so, he has confined himself in human experience, even though as the Word he cannot be confined. To heal, he must assume what is wounded. To reconcile, he must join what has been put asunder. He has chosen to assume her sin-sick humanness to cleanse it of its pollution, to draw from it its poison, to cool its fever. She will watch in horror as he is victimized by his own loving decision to follow this through to his death. As she accompanies him, something in her will be put to death; something will die. This is the meaning of the Lenten journey. Without the relationship of Lover and beloved, the time can degenerate into a spiritual basic training camp assignment, a grin-and-bear-it, gotta-go-through-it forced march.

The season begins in the desert. The scripture says the Spirit drives him there. Together, he and the woman-in-love face temptation. The tempter suggests: Satisfy yourself. Turn stones into bread. Work a holy trick. Hide under the cloak of religion. Together they reply, No, not a holy trick. Just a centering on the word of God as my food. A second temptation: Then throw yourself down, for God will catch you... And a second refusal: Yes, he will-but not on a dare. And still a third temptation: I will give you everything ... if you worship me ... And the final refusal: Begone ... God alone is worthy of worship. These temptations are not just those of Jesus. They are ours. When we read them, locked in our communion with him, we feel the strength to withstand them because we are not alone. Their antidote is a chaste focus on the Word, an obedient listening for God's will over the demand that God do what I demand, and a radical poverty in worshiping only God in my life. These radical choices, as non-negotiable, clean out the house of the soul.

The strength of these decisions comes from fasting, prayer, and almsgiving — the three ancient balms for the sick soul. What is amazing is how these three really antidote the three poisons suggested in the scriptural temptations. Fasting puts boundaries on the self-satisfaction that comes from eating, the most common of human activities. Lack of moderation in caring for the physical dimension of ourselves can wreak havoc. Obesity and alcoholic addiction are but two examples. Fasting in Lent is not primarily for losing weight. Fasting is for restoring boundaries to my self-indulgence, yet a side result will almost certainly be a healthy weight loss. Because the judgment is clouded as a result of food or alcohol addiction, a person caught in obesity or alcoholism needs the help of another to make good judgments. Allowing someone we trust to walk with us for a while will help us get the excess under control and give us a sense of confidence and support. Left on our own we fall into despair and hopelessness. We can't seem to make it work, so we give up and throw it overboard.

Fasting is simpler than many think. I eat a bit of fruit and toast for breakfast, make sure my main meal at noon is moderate in its portions, and have a bit of soup and salad for supper. For those who have lost a sense of moderation this can sound quite sparse. In reality it is eating to live rather than living to eat, and that makes a big difference. On meatless days (Ash Wednesday and the Fridays of Lent in the Catholic and Orthodox traditions) the main meal is meatless. In our culture it has been discovered that what appears to be hunger is often a cry for water. We are chronically dehydrated, thus susceptible to infections of various kinds. A very meaningful Lenten practice can be to drink eight glasses of water daily to remedy this condition alongside our fasting.

The second temptation would have us dare God to prove things to us. There is a blatant arrogance in this expectation. It is as though we are playing a tune and God must dance to it. In reality this attitude comes from a fevered, puffed-up ego. Prayer releases the hot air. Praying is not saying prayers. The first step of prayer is showing up, sitting down, and shutting up. Many of us don't get this far. We show up perhaps, we may sit down, or kneel, and then we start talking. I suspect at some point God yawns. The step of silence is crucial. We come before the burning bush and remove our sandals. This imagery reveals a divestiture, a putting off of what might protect me from God. To look at God looking at me is terrifying in the beginning, but it must be done. That loving look, totally accepting of me in my wretchedness, creates a humbleness in me that is very pleasing to God. Once there is an understanding that God loves me regardless of my condition, I can just be there as I am. I don't have to make excuses, or rattle on, or say many words. I just look and know. Words might follow, but they follow, they do not lead.

The third temptation, to possess everything I want, is cured by almsgiving. This practice is more than putting a coin in the beggar's hand. Almsgiving is facing the fact of my own radical poverty, the fact that I have nothing of myself, and all I have is a gift. Almsgiving is just being kind. Once this is again deeply owned, the extra items in my closet or on my shelves call to be given to someone who has need of them. The gospel nowhere demands that we become destitute. What is asked is that we share what we have with others. If this were done, poverty would disappear. Consumerism is the opposite of this sharing. I go shopping not to get what I need, but to find out what I should want. I get what I want and have so many of them that I forget what I have. Then I go out and add more until I have so much I need a bigger space to store it all in. I am depressed because I need to take care of it all, protect it all, and lock it all up. The gospel calls us to live simply so that others can simply live. This can mean living with great beauty. We have what we need and so do those around us. If they don't have what they need, we band with others to help provide. Those who know that this is an area in their lives needing radical change, will find interesting company. More and more families, executives, and professional people are determined to live simply. They are banding together to help one another work out a lifestyle that is more simple and generous. It is clear that this agenda is not a matter of pious wishful thinking. This is radical housecleaning of the mind, heart, and soul.

Lent is approximately six weeks. About halfway through, the Church is given a preview of coming attractions. With her eyes firmly on the One she loves, she suddenly sees him change before her eyes. The transfiguration of Jesus on Mount Tabor is presented to her. This is a view of the hidden mystery carried in the sacred humanity of Jesus. Lest we think it is nothing but the privilege of a select few, it is in reality not just about him, but about ourselves. His hidden beauty is our own. We are only too aware of our brokenness, our meanness, our sin. What we do not see is our hidden beauty. So hidden from us is this reality that we do not believe it exists. Yet it is there, and God sees it and delights in it. It is precisely this beauty that we profane when we act in a way unworthy of who we are.

The final week of Lent is known as Holy Week. The week opens with the fleeting triumph of Palm Sunday. With her eyes still on the One she loves, the Church rides in with him humbly on a donkey. This description is significant for the Church, for it focuses anew on her servant identity in the world, this in stark contrast to elitism. The shouts and praise ringing in her ears leave a lump in her stomach. Well she knows that it is only a matter of days when the shouts will call for his death.

In Jerusalem there is a sealed stone gateway. Outside it, there are many Jewish graves. It is believed that this is the gateway that the Messiah will come through when he arrives, and many Jews request to be buried nearby to be on hand to welcome him.

This is the gate Jesus entered on Palm Sunday. It has since been sealed.

Wednesday of Holy Week has been called "Spy Wednesday." In the scriptures of the day the betrayal of Judas is read. Rather than pass this by as something too bad that happened to Jesus, we would do well to remember that what happens to him happens to us, and reflect on the betrayals of our own lives. There are those we have suffered, and those we have inflicted on others. Both can be dealt with only by the courage we gather by seeing them reflected in his eyes — in an immense sea of mercy. Only in this bigger context can we gather the strength to forgive ourselves. Without this sea of mercy we can become locked in the windowless darkroom of our own guilt.

The Thursday, Friday, and Saturday of Holy Week are known as the Sacred Triduum or the Sacred Three Days. They are the highpoint of the year, and culminate with Easter, the greatest feast of the Christian year. Once again, the deepest significance of these days can be plumbed only when we approach them in the communion of the Church with her Beloved. If this bond is broken, we find ourselves simply remembering past things that unfortunately happened to Jesus.

The first of these three days, Holy Thursday, is the commemoration of the Last Supper. This day will be especially significant to churches with a strong sacramental tradition. For these churches the Eucharist is the final gift of the Incarnate Word. It is the culmination of both the Incarnation and the Passion. In the Eucharist, the Word that has joined itself to our humanness finds a way to feed us as long as the world lasts. The Eucharistic bread is the final sign of this self-giving love.

This sacrament is given on the night before Jesus dies. Because this celebration takes place in the shadow of Good Friday, it is muted, and will be celebrated more fully in a feast of its own after Easter. We will reflect on its meaning more in that context. There is a touching commemoration on this night that takes place only during this week. When the Holy Thursday Eucharist is over, the consecrated bread is carried in procession around the church. This recalls how Jesus went from court to court after his arrest, finally spending the night in a Roman prison, probably a pit in the ground, as excavations have shown. The Eucharist is placed at a side altar for the night, and the main altar is stripped of all its covering. Vigil is kept until midnight, after which the Eucharist is reserved in the sacristy The church is then darkened and totally empty. Again the significance is deliberate and touching. The symbolism is moving for those who remain to watch. But again, its meaning depends on the communion of the Church and its Beloved central to this action. Genuine sacramental action is in truth the word acted out. As an active word, sacraments are one with the word read to us from the scripture. The Church is going through this with the One she loves, and the One she loves both speaks and acts.

Good Friday dawns silent and somber. At some time in the afternoon, usually at three o'clock, the church gathers. Barefooted, the priest enters, and falls prostrate before the bare altar where he remains for a time. The Church kneels. The passion is then read, the Word is preached, and this is followed by prayers for different peoples of the world: non-believers, the Jews, those in civil office, travelers, and refugees. In solemn procession, the cross is then carried in. Silently the congregation processes up, one by one, to kiss the cross. The Eucharist from Holy Thursday night is then brought in and communion is distributed. There is no Mass. The cross is placed where latecomers can honor it, the altar is again stripped, and the church darkened. The Eucharist is again removed from the church. The only light is near the bare cross.

This is what takes place ritually, symbolically. What does it mean? Why is the church in mourning when these events happened 2000 years ago, when they are over and done with? Or are they? Once again we need to recall the fact that the woman-in-love, the Church, is bringing her reality to him as well as recalling his sufferings for her. The gospels recall his agony in a garden while his followers fell asleep. She is all too aware of his continued agony in the garden spots of the world and the concrete jungles of many cities, where his followers squirm under the pressure of those who regard religion, both true and fake, as pious opiate. She recalls his merciless scourging, aware that his body still is beaten bloody in the bodies of countless women and children who are objects of someone's sexual desires or rage. In the crowning with thorns and mockery she recognizes the thorn helmet's modern design, crushed down on the heads of prisoners of conscience who languish in hidden prisons because they dared to speak the truth; on the heads of children as they are shown how to kill and how to hate as a way of life, as minds are twisted by fundamentalist extremism to self-destruct in the name of God. This is happening to *her* now, to her world, not just to him way back then. She recalls him dragging an instrument of execution through public streets, stumbling, falling, and falling again. But she knows it still goes on in addicts who drag themselves back to the bottle, or to the fix, or to the brothel, or to the casino. She watches in horror as he is tortured with nails piercing the hands that blessed and feet that carried him from place to place. He is hung up like a piece of meat to lure vultures. His arms are outstretched like a mother crying out to her lost children and expecting them to jump into her arms. Faces and names pass before her mind's eye ... the death camps, Bosnia, Mi Lai, Rwanda ... boat people, refugees with no place to go, children too weak from hunger to stand up, the line at the abortion clinic, the shocked faces at the HIV testing site. They are all crucified on different crosses.

And she can't take them down. For she knows she takes turns *being hung up herself* and *doing the crucifying* by her complicity in systemic evil. This is the agony of her reflection. She cannot separate herself from him, and he cannot, will not, separate himself from his body, the Church, for better or worse. The purpose of the symbolism is to break her heart, to wring from it the last vestiges of the idolatrous whoring that has pierced his own heart, leaving it hanging open on the cross, as Catherine of Siena says, like a window opened, never to be shuttered.

Holy Saturday dawns and feels like a day suspended between death and life. The Easter lilies are quietly prepared for evening, and last instructions might be given to those to be baptized. At dusk the church gathers to keep vigil, to keep watch for her Beloved. Her mind is numb, for nothing is rational about all this. Her faith holds her mind in its embrace, rocking it as it shakes its head and moans. The community gathers in total darkness and silence. At the appointed time a new fire is struck from flint and the huge Easter candle is lit. From it candles held by each person are lit and in the spreading light the Exultet is sung — a peon of joy usually sung solo by a voice that rings through the church. The lights burst on and the Gloria, silent all during Lent, is sung with abandon. After the first readings of the resurrection, the baptisms take place, usually by immersion if possible, and the newly baptized process forward in their white robes, like people beginning their lives all over again. The liturgy continues with a wild joy not to be equaled by the second Mass of Easter on Sunday, which pales in comparison. The Holy Saturday vigil and celebration have become the major Easter celebration, the celebration for lovers.

What is all of this trying to say? A lot. What is being celebrated is not just an event that happened long ago. Christians believe that the resurrection is a historical event. What is being celebrated is the fact that death does not, and will not, have the last word — for Jesus, for us, and for the world. The basis for this faith is something that cannot be proved. It can only be trusted. Those who believe this without doubt take their chances on the faith of millions who have gone before them. Those who choose not to believe take their chances too. Each of us has to be prepared to be wrong. We have to decide how we want to take our chances. This is what faith means. It is not irrational, but it cannot be explained with scientific proof. It is a knowing that comes from loving. We owe respect to those struggling to make that choice.

The Last Idol

Your vacant stare greets me

when I look in the mirror.

I know you, behind that grin.

I watch for you, sure you will show.

Eyes that will not see, and ears plugged,

You siphon off my attentiveness

whining for the sick scent of incense.

Serpent in the shadow of the sick-self
Come out!

Why do you entrance me
with your hollow rattle
and a flailing tail
your head already crushed
beneath a wounded foot.

I owe my homage elsewhere.

C.M. Streeter, O.P., 1983

Easter:
the Season of Promise

Where It's All Headed

*T*he white-gold of this season comes upon the church like frozen light. The wild joy is dilated, the church so wide-eyed she hardly seems to blink. Signs of spring bursting everywhere in nature usually accompany the interior jubilation. It is the season of the untranslatable "Alleluia!" and the time of daffodils bowing to strains of Vivaldi's *Springtime* sounding in the mind while you are driving down the street. Visually the huge Easter candle dominates church sanctuaries, shorter acolytes stretching with persistence until its wick bursts into flame.

There is no trace of hypocrisy in this joy on the part of those who know themselves to be sinners. Rather, the sinners are fixated on a sight more compelling than their own winding cloths, more fascinating than decay. Easter is about a change beyond your wildest dreams. Easter is seeing a promise fulfilled before your very eyes.

Easter is about the body. Everyone the world over knows the body will succumb to death. It will stop moving, stop breathing, stop feeling. There will be no more laughing, or crying, or holding, or kissing. Death is the monster in the human closet, always lurking there where one sleeps and rises. It waits for all, and comes out in due time. Easter is about beating the monster, breaking its power. Easter is about delivery of a promise, the keeping of a pledge. Easter is about the transformation of the human, and it begins with the body, the physical dimension of the human being.

Many religions believe that upon death the spirit of the person roams or goes to a place of peace and joy. Christians come to the table of world religions with a preposterous report, based on eyewitnesses. They claim to have real news. The body is not lost after all. It may become earth, disintegrate into its elements, but no matter. It will be back. That same body, but different. The story of its journey is clear to see, yet beautiful and new, as if the DNA touched some celestial circuit and got lit up. Easter is about transformed humanness, inside out, and outside in. What is more, Christians claimed to have seen this transformation, and later died rather than retract what they had said. Either we are reading accounts of some mass hysteria, or something happened that we don't understand, and it's not a trivial matter.

The resurrection accounts of the risen Jesus were not the way to go for a new upstart religion to get off the ground. Ridicule does not make for converts. Yet with calm steadiness the disciples tell the story of a dead man, brutally executed, who returns to his friends and shows them a real body, a real person, new and different, but himself. All too familiar with the supposed finality of death, the disciples react with fear and disbelief.

Easter is about a revelation. It is about a realized promise, not only for Jesus, but for all humans. It reveals that the Love that holds all of creation in its hand will not be robbed. Death will not destroy what Love has made to be. And when the human creature dies in Love, death has met its match and will itself be destroyed. We did not know this. We could dream it in the ancient cults and multiple incarnations of ancient traditions, but to have a communal experience of it? That is another matter. This is the Christian claim. They claim to have been shown what happens to the human being who dies in Love.

Computer graphics can create effects that defy the eye. They can imagine the human body transformed into energy to be reassembled in another location in a "Beam me up, Scotty!" scenario. But make no mistake. We are not talking here about a resuscitated Jesus. We are talking about a transformed, different Jesus, the same but at times not recognized, as if our current vision can't get it. The promise the resurrection brings is that we are seeing our future when we gaze into Easter.

Deep within the consciousness of the human is the intuition that death is not the end, that there is something else. Different cultures express this in varied ways, from the food found in tombs to the worship of ancestors. Christians claim to have the final piece of the puzzle. They present to an incredulous world a revelation of where it's all heading, and, in particular, what the future of the human being is.

Is it really so outlandish to think that our love, caught up in *that* Love, is going to change our very substance — our DNA — our molecular structure? That our physicality can be recreated from restructured atoms under the guidance of a power and presence from the depths of our own souls? That the spirit part of our humanness will now dictate to the physical, giving it capabilities we do not experience in our present condition? Why not?

The mystery of Easter, in order to make a statement to sin and death itself, lasts forty days plus ten. The church's use of time to make a point is not lost in this season. After forty days the Ascension is celebrated, a feast that passes many Christians by unnoticed. Jesus is taken up into heaven, the scriptures say. Good for him, some might say. But for the more thoughtful, this is no minor feast.

If the resurrection points to our future, so does the Ascension. The woman-in-love cannot separate herself from him. She knows that what happens with him is his promise to her. The Ascension means that her substance, her human physicality to which he has indissolubly united himself, has been carried into the very heart of God. This is her destiny, nothing less. No wonder the angels ask the gaping disciples why they are standing staring into the heavens. This mystery is enough to rivet our souls such that we too need to be reminded that we still have work to do. The realization is enough to make you lose interest in your job, your family, your car, and your bills.

This season unfolds with a sensitivity akin to caring for a victim of shock. Once the disciples stop looking up into the future they obediently go into a type of retreat to come to terms with all that has been shown them. They go to the upper room for ten days. Not much is said about this time except that the mother of Jesus was with them, a seemingly insignificant detail. Yet it is a detail that matches perfectly another scripture observation about her, that "Mary treasured all these words and pondered them in her heart" (Lk. 2:19). She is the image of the Church in the aftershock of what she has learned about the plan. Her instructions are to stay in Jerusalem until the Advocate comes, the one to plead her cause. But what that meant she could only guess. After all that she had experienced, common sense would have dictated that a time-out was needed. So they waited.

Jesus had told them that it was necessary for him to go away. Only then would the Spirit come, the One who would make everything they had heard clear. What they had seen and heard, what they had experienced, had turned their world upside down. They viewed themselves, their world, their destiny, and their God differently. He had seen to that. But they were very aware of their sinfulness and fear. Now he was gone. What next?

It isn't hard for us as a Church to identify with the helplessness of these disciples. If anyone had the right to be in spiritual shock, they did. And so they hid out. They waited and prayed, and the mother of Jesus was there with them. They needed to be reborn so they needed a mother. And déjà vu, true to pattern, the Divine transposes the theme from the Spirit overshadowing the maid to the Spirit overshadowing the community. Like drunkards, high on the Spirit's wine, they stumble out of their hiding place, and no one can shut them up. The scene is of former cowards transformed into preachers. Lit by the Spirit's fire they remember indeed, things become clear indeed. There is a new birth, and I think Mary must have looked down into the gathered crowd in the street and laughed a delightful laugh.

This is the fullness of the Easter season, the season of promise. There is the promise of death's power being broken. There is the revelation of the transformed humanness that he comes to show them. He carefully folds the winding cloths of his grave, laying them aside as though a part of his life were being laid aside, a part he will no longer need. There is the sight of them all gazing up toward wherever he is taking their humanness, joined irrevocably to it as he is. There is the blast of the Spirit's wind, clearing out the final debris of their hearts and firing them up to spread the message far and wide. This is the Easter season, no less for us than for them. It was necessary that he go away indeed. But again, make no mistake: Removing his new physical presence from their clinging grasp, to allow the Spirit to have its way with them, does not mean he is gone. On the contrary, he says elsewhere, "I am with you always, to the end of the age" (Mt. 28:20b). So he is here, he is not dead; and that Spirit, by fire, is still forging witnesses from cowards.

Easter

Wooden bed of "yes"
your arms release
the Sleeper.

Awake
He leaves behind
the journey-shoes of time.

But flesh he takes
singing
into glory!

Wakened One
tend us
walking weary in our worn-out shoes.

Quicken us
with your Spirit-word
and teach our flesh to sing!

C.M. Streeter, O.P., 1983

Post-Paschal Feasts: the Season of Insight

Three Persons, Two Hearts, and One Body

*T*his season opens like an afterglow. The weekdays return to the vibrant green of the Ordinary Time briefly begun after Epiphany, except when a martyr is remembered and the red vestments attest to the shedding of blood, or white recalls the baptism of a virgin or confessor of the faith. What is celebrated in this afterglow?

Immediately after Pentecost the Feast of the Trinity appears, like fire on the mountain. The mystery of the Triune God, One and Three, has become an embarrassment for many preachers. What does one say? For many preachers as well as congregations, this doctrine has become obtuse, locked in the abstraction of theory that never has been transposed into meaningful language. In reality, the mystery is utterly concrete - it is the fountainhead of all that is, all that has any existence whatsoever.

The dynamic fountain of Being that we call God pours itself out in active Love. Although male terms are used to refer to it, the Father is continually giving birth. This mysterious Father is the hidden heart of the Godhead. From the Father all comes in a constant stream of merciful compassion. So central is this loving mercy, identifying the very heart of God, that even the justice of God is within it, and a form of it. They must never be considered separate, one from the other.

This merciful compassion longs to express itself, and in an act of outflowing love does so. The expression of God is total. God empties God's self out, as it were. In a burst of self-giving love, this expression, true God of true God, is the Word of God. The Word of God is the "Son" of the Father, offspring of the womb of this infinite mercy. The Word knows itself in the mirror that is the Father, and this knowing burns with the Love that binds the two in one. This Love, because it is God's Love, is true God of true God. This Holy Spirit of self-giving and delighting Love embraces and flows between Father and Son, Source and Word. Notice that already in the longing to express, the Love is there. So the Spirit proceeds from the Father just as the Son does. In fact, contrary to the understanding of many, there is, in our temporal manner of speaking, a moment in which the Spirit precedes the Son as the very Love that brings forth the Word. Our temporal sequence simply does not apply.

This dance of Love, each of the Three flowing into the Other, is a total oneness. Yet the oneness is triadic while at the same time being One. When faced with this mystery, the human mind functions as it usually does. When we distinguish something from something else, we inadvertently also *separate* what we have distinguished. In dealing with this mystery, revealed to humans only through Jesus who refers to this triadic-yet-one God, we need to restrain the usual pattern of the mind. We need to instead intentionally keep the Three as One in the midst of distinguishing them one from the other. For the Source is not the Expression, and both Source and Expression can be distinguished from dynamic Love. The relationship is such, however, that we cannot speak of one without the other. There is no Song if there is no Singer. There is no Singer if there is no Song, and there can be no Song if there is no Singing. Such is the Mystery.

Rather than be dismissed as an abstraction, this Mystery is the very ground of all our human relationships. We need only to reflect on our own activity to be in touch with it. I give birth to thoughts, inner words. They are me, thinking. In my limited human way, I love my own thoughts. The pattern is there. I come to know you, and I begin to love you. We marry, and from our knowing each other intimately in love, another comes to be. The pattern is there. The supernova collapses. From it comes the stuff of new life directed by some unifying force. The pattern is there.

We need to find new words to preach and teach this Mystery. The time of triangles and shamrocks may be past. Instead I suggest a very simple concrete visual image to help us. The candle is used in worship across the world. It may be useful for us to reflect simply on its *flame*. We know there is a flame because we see its light, or we feel its heat. There is no heat without the flame, nor is there light without the flame. Yet we can talk about the heat distinct from the light, and the light distinct from the flame and the heat. What is key to this image is the *relationship* that differs, while the essential is shared by all.

Reflection on this Mystery has the amazing effect of putting the human mind in right proportion to faith. The mind is the distinctive human identifying trait. Human intelligence is a marvel. It is the imprint in the human of the knowing God. Surely the mind should not be told to shut down when it comes to the Divine Mystery Itself. Yet when confronted with the Triadic Mystery, the human mind stops, stunned. Faith brings it to the point of ascent. It can make the judgment *that* God is One yet Three, but not *how*. To the human mind in its earthly sojourn, the Trinity is a type of koan. The mind stands stupefied before something it cannot fully grasp. We need go no further to find the appropriate posture of the mind before what faith presents. The mind must remove its sandals. This image suggests that discursive reasoning is put on hold. One way to be sure the Mystery known is authentic is that the mind cannot fully grasp it, for to do so, the mind would be God. This safeguards the distinction between Creator and creature. The Creator is the One who is. We are the ones who are not, except by being given existence from this Holy One.

No sooner has the church celebrated the coming of the Word in our flesh, and its life, death, and resurrection among us, and the final sending of that Spirit who will return everything to the Father, when the Feast of the Three in One focuses our attention on the Mystery behind it all. Being "behind it all" means, of course, being the source of all of it, but also the end of all of it, for we will find ourselves back to where we originated.

While we are still blinking at the Triadic Mystery, the fire on the mountain, the Church takes up some unfinished business. During Holy Week, the celebration of the gift of the Eucharist on Holy Thursday night was muted by the coming passion on Good Friday. Now the Church returns to this love-gift of the Word in our flesh to celebrate it in the afterglow of the Paschal Mystery. Traditionally in early times, the Thursday after the Feast of the Trinity was the celebration of Corpus Christi, or the Body of Christ. Recently the celebration has been moved to a Sunday to allow more of the faithful to be part of the celebration, since weekday Eucharist is not an option for many.

The Eucharistic presence of the risen Christ has been a point of discussion ecumenically for many years. Recently quite a bit of agreement was reached in the Lutheran/Catholic dialogue. For our purposes here, we will focus on the meaning of what is celebrated, and the significance that meaning has for the ordinary life of the Christian.

Theological arguments aside, this celebration means that the One who has joined the Godhead to our humble humanness has found a way to nourish the new life bought for us at the price of blood. The Eucharist is food, and food is a "word" all its own. To come to know someone better, one eats with the person. We have lunch. It is almost as though the act of eating is signing the relating that is going on, person to person.

This is a feast of the body. It is a celebration of divine/human intimacy. There is no sacramental "magic" here. There *is* human touch, person-to-person contact. A risen, transformed human person makes contact with a sinful pilgrim, struggling to walk in Christian discipleship. That contact, simple eating, slowly inches the pilgrim into his or her own transformation. The Eucharist is what effects human transformation and healing. The Eucharist is the concretization of the scriptural word, "Abide in me as I abide in you" (Jn. 15:4a). So simple is the sacramental sign that a child is simply told that Jesus wants to come and be with us. We invite him in, and he comes to help us be all we can be. In contrast to the regular food we eat, which becomes part of us, this food transforms us into *itself.* We become capable of resurrected life, won for us by the very Love that feeds us.

For those who understand the full meaning of this feast, this is not a feast of Jesus merely celebrated in the ritual of the liturgy. This is the feast of the total Body of Christ, Head and members, and the ongoing conversion needed as he lives her life with her in this world, Body to body.

For the woman-in-love, the Church, this is an intimacy beyond the sexual intimacy of marriage, and indeed, it is this very communion in love that marriage signifies. But the meaning doesn't stop here. The ritual celebration of the Body of Christ is one thing. The reality that it ritualizes is another. The risen Christ is not communing with the Christian in splendid isolation. The risen Christ, for better or worse, is forever married to a body called the Church.

They are one. This human institution, this human sign in the world, is shockingly sinful. She has literally been the death of him. In her better moments she brings him immense joy in those who suffer heroically in their struggle for justice, for peace, and for integrity. He delights in her holy ones, the saints. He is irrevocably joined to her leaders, who at times get drunk on power and betray him all over again. But not all those in office are such. There are those faithful shepherds who have indeed laid down their lives for the sheep. Yet the risen One is faithful to the union he has effected with this humanness, until he brings his love, the Church, safely home.

The Friday and Saturday after Corpus Christi bring the quiet feasts of two hearts. On Friday the heart of Jesus is celebrated, and on Saturday, the heart of his mother. We celebrate the Sacred Heart of Jesus, the heart of the Incarnate Word, and the Immaculate Heart of Mary, the heart of a simple human woman who said yes to the divine plan. Are these mere Catholic fetishes? What insights might these two celebrations bring us?

The heart is the seat of motivation and love. We speak of loving someone with all our heart, or putting our heart into a project. We certainly are not merely talking about a physical organ. We are referring to the deepest core of the person, the center from which comes all they do.

It is significant that in the scriptural account of the passion, the heart of Jesus is pierced. It is opened, and the scripture says that blood and water came out of the open heart. Water is the sign of cleansing and blood is the sign of life, of healing, of strength.

Someone with outstretched arms now has a wide-open heart, from which comes cleansing and life. What are we being told here?

Jesus is the revelation of God, the image of the invisible God. This is no way for a God to present himself. To our minds, there should be fire and sounding trumpets and smoke, and perhaps lightning and an earthquake. In fact, the scriptural account comes close. At the death of Jesus there is darkness and earthquake and, most significantly, *the temple curtain is torn in two.* The real God has come from behind the curtain. No more hiding. The real God, the God of tender love and unbelievable mercy is hanging up on the hill. An announcement is being made: Come see the God you didn't expect. Come see a God weak with love. Come see what you are worth to your God who becomes vulnerable to evil to save you from its sting. Come see a God with his heart hanging open. Come — hide. Climb in where the water will wash you and the blood will heal you and revive you and give you new life. Come, see my powerful arms are pinned helpless. Come hide in my heart. I thirst — not for water, but for yourself. Come. Do not be afraid.

This heart is the mercy seat. This is where we go to escape the rightful wrath of God. In this heart the justice lion lies down with the lamb. In the midst of all this the heart of the Christian cries out, "Will the real God please stand up? Once and for all, who are you?" And God is not deaf.

Christians who are familiar with their scriptures are given multiple images of God. It is important to remember that these images develop from one

God among many, to the one and only God. Then there is the God of Sinai thundering, and the God of the Song of Solomon (Song of Songs) panting with desire for the beloved. Jesus has been designated as the image of the invisible God. This reference from the Christian scriptures should give us pause. Perhaps the time has come for a full and more accurate revelation of the "real" God. If this is so, then the Crucified is a wonder to behold. The various scriptures do indeed present God to us. But this is a scandal - the scandal of the cross. Could it be that we are being told that the very heart of God is not wrath and justice, not unapproachable holiness, but heartfelt mercy? Tender compassion? Open welcome to the likes of us?

Heart to heart, what is the meaning of celebrating the heart of the woman who mothered the Christ? After all, hers is but a feminine human heart, no more. Could it be that in honoring her heart we are honoring the heartfelt motivation of every human woman and man who has opened a human life to the power of God? We give Purple Hearts to soldiers who show valor in battle. Is this a form of honor for another kind of battle-the kind where the enemy is crippling fear and doubt and uncertainty? Is this one more move to make sure the human element is not neglected?

Like the Eucharist, Mary has been an ecumenical bone of contention. But recent studies have shown a remarkable ecumenical interest in this woman who plays a critical role in the plan to redeem us. No goddess, but a human figure who makes it clear that God intends to work things out with human cooperation, not by means of a shotgun wedding in spite of us. Hers was a faith-filled and faithful heart. Is she perhaps given to us as the model for our human response to God? The humble maid of Nazareth was one of us. What she did under the influence of grace is how we too are dealt with - we are asked to respond to God through the influence of grace in our lives. Is our role as clear without her? Is the Church's role as clear without her?

With these celebrations this season of the soul comes to a close. It is now June, and summer is upon Christians in a large part of the world. The seed has been planted and has burst forth in all its glory. Now it is time to look for the fruit, for the harvest.

Trinity

My tent flap hung in the heat
limp.
Hospitality hunched inside
dozing
lulled by buzzing flies.
A breeze stirred
bringing three guests.

Mouth and macho
introduced the trio,
never-silent heart hustler.
Silent and sad
held out his hands —
waiting wounded.
Loving clown,
smiling through tear-stained greasepaint
promising life.

A playful child stirs
and Sara laughs.

C.M. Streeter, O.P., 1980

Ordinary Time:
the Season of Integration

A Most Extraordinary Mission

*T*his season of the soul enters in verdant green, the color of lush growth, flourishing, and productivity. The greening that is Ordinary Time is anything but ordinary. It is the season for integrating all that has gone before. The longing of Advent that gave way to the coming of the Word in Christmastide, and the further revealing of that Word in ever-wider contexts including the spectacle of the passion, death, and resurrection, is now blended into a burst of beauty under the Spirit's orchestration.

The themes in this verdant symphony are drawn from the Spirit's activity in the beloved, the woman-in-love that is the Church. It is the time for her to become fruitful. It is the time for evidence of their relationship. It is time for healthy harvesting from the lives of Christians who have walked the talk and lived into the Word.

What then is this most extraordinary mission? It is to weave out of the everyday a garment of glory, a wedding garment. Ordinary Time is the opportunity for the woman-in-love to go to the loom. There the shuttle will go in and out: the "in" of receiving, drinking in, tolerance, and listening; and the "out" of offering, care, and challenge to a culture that is often self-obsessed. It is the time to weave all of the colors together, to create patterns distinct to the church's life in this world, at this time. It will not do to wear old threadbare garments from the past. It will not do to wear the regal robes that rank you with the elite. It's time to weave the wedding garment, the robe for union, for intimacy and identity. The Church, this woman-in-love, receives her directions for the garment from the Spirit, and the material is the stuff of her ordinary day — her wonder, her questions, her insights, her thinking, her judgments, her decisions. The loom is her location, and it could be Afghanistan in its dark agony, or Rome in its gleaming gold. It could be Baghdad in its front-page crimson, or Haiti in its earthy brown. She will weave, and the garment will take shape.

Ordinary Time typically extends from June to November, a full half of the year. From December through May the gaze of the community is on him — on her need for him, her joy in his coming, her wonder at his presence, her horror at his sufferings, and her marveling at his transformation through death and what all this might mean for her. Now the gaze turns toward herself, and her response to him. She will deck herself out in her wedding clothes to await his return.

The Word does not return void. It has been at work. It has effect. The results of the Word working in the world will be seen first in her, for she is the first fruits of his reign. She is the extension of himself into time. She knows he will not be known except through her mysterious presence in the world, hidden though that might be. Indissolubly joined to him in the common humanness he has taken on himself, she struggles to be true to him, to be faithful, yet is often sinful, fearful, and stubborn.

This time will unfold with the Word, constantly encouraging, chiding, warning, reminding, reassuring, and affirming her as she struggles to give birth to substantive new growth in her children. She needs to be called again and again to be hospitable and welcoming in the inclusive way he modeled for her. This means the struggle to be open to all, including the most despicable and rejected of society. He will, through his word, remind her where her strength comes from. She will need to be reminded that her arrogance is but wind producing nothing. Over and over again he himself will nourish her to be able to carry out her mission, to do this, to be this, in the midst of human desecration and degradation. She will baptize, confirm, and offer communion because that is what he continues to do.

She needs to be called over and over again to the healing he wants to effect in broken human lives. This will mean the forgiving seventy times seven times, whether this involves the prostitute or the wayward priest, the abusive husband or the alcoholic. She will be called to be at the bedside of those preparing to die. She will need to be there, ready to look death in the face with them, quietly reminding them it will not have the last word — he will. She will absolve and anoint because he aches to do so.

She will need to give birth to new leaders, to those who will mirror his priesthood and their own as the community gathers to "do this in remembrance of me" (1 Cor. 11:24b). She will bless with joy the unions

87

of those who are going to sign his self-giving love day in and day out in the sweaty work of building a marriage and founding a family. None of this will she do alone. She has no meaning aside from him, and what she does has meaning only because she gives him a continual humanness to keep doing what he wants to do. She is nothing, yet everything, for he has determined to act in the world in tandem with her, for better or for worse. By his own determination he is stuck with her.

This union between the Christ and the church is an agony and an ecstasy beyond any soap opera. It is the drama of the centuries, and it goes on. In his own words, it will last until the end of time. It will last until she has a clear face, free of the blemishes that pockmark her beauty. It will last until she becomes a clear transparent sign of him. For he is not tucked off in some heaven wishing her luck. He is in her, breathing and enduring the pangs of continual labor until she brings forth the fruit of his living and dying, the fruit of his loving.

Ordinary Time is the time of weddings and ordinations, of graduations and new jobs. It is the time of vacations and travel, of yard work and gardening. It is the time of warm nights and soft rains, of visiting Grandma and burying Grandpa. It is the time of raking leaves and picking pumpkins, of buckling down to the familiar school schedule.

In all of this hustle and bustle of human encounter the Spirit groans. Relationships are mended, deepened, broken, and mended again. The woman-in-love knows tears and laughter, grief and despair, wonder and weariness. This is the Church, the *real*

Church. Her inner structure is institutional, but she is slowly learning not to wear it on the outside like a crustacean.

Several feasts are celebrated during this Ordinary Time, and they are noteworthy. They are strategically placed to help the community to remember, lest they forget what they are about. The first two of these remembrances are related. August 6 recalls the Transfiguration of Jesus on Mount Tabor, when he gave three of his apostles a glimpse of what his sacred humanity veiled. Why, we might ask, is this remembrance placed right in the middle of summer, halfway through Ordinary Time? It makes sense if we think of him reminding her not only of his identity, but also of her own reality, her own inner beauty, the beauty he won for her at great cost. The second highlight is the celebration of the Assumption of the Mother of God. There has never been recorded in the Church any honoring of the gravesite of Mary. Instead, from ancient times the Church has believed she experienced in Mary what we all shall experience — the transformation of her humanness and being reunited with her son. Again we might ask, why this remembrance now? Carefully placed in the midst of the busyness of summer, these celebrations are like a pause that refreshes. We are caught just for a moment and focused on the end of it all. We are reminded of where it is all heading. We are given an eschatological reminder.

September brings the first signs of autumn and the leaves begin to dry up and fall. The lush green of summer begins to give way to the somber hues that turn the trees into palettes of color. Right in the midst of September there is the celebration of a tree. September 14 is the celebration of the Exaltation of the Cross. Nowhere near Lent, this remembrance sounds a somber note in the midst of autumn beauty, a note of tragedy. Only Christians celebrate an instrument of execution. The horror of the cross is held up before us six months before Lent, in the midst of Ordinary Time. For strict monastic orders it signals the beginning of a time of self-discipline, anticipating Lent by a half year, and calling these celibate lovers into an early fasting routine that makes sense only to lovers. For the majority of the Church it is but the sounding of a chord that announces the double theme of the Paschal Mystery, the dying and the rising, the ebb and flow of the cosmos, of all of nature, brought to visibility in the dying and rising of her Beloved.

For children, October means the celebration of Halloween and the fun of trick or treat. The origin of this festival is generally linked to the Druids. It falls on the night before the first of November, the Feast of All the Saints. The medieval church was all too aware of demons. Viruses and birth defects, effects that as yet had no scientific explanation, were often attributed to demonic influence. November 1st was the celebration of all those whose struggle was over. We remember the holy ones of God, those whose names and lives were honored publicly, and those mothers and fathers, grandparents and teens, statesmen and sailors, and doctors and housewives whose names we do not know. They've made it home. They rest in God. They are like some holy harvest. But then there are the demons. They're still busy. They try to trip us up. But these holy ones got by. They're safe. So we make fun of the losers. The demons get trounced. Thus begins the custom of dressing up in ghoulish disguises and partying the day before November first, the holy evening, "Hallow's Eve" — all in Ordinary Time. Then on November 1 the masks come off. Our true faces shine out, radiant and holy.

All of this is in preparation for the grand climax of the year, which will end just before the first Sunday of Advent. The liturgical year ends with a solemn remembrance of the kingship of Christ. In a time of triumphalism, this feast fed a sick superiority complex in the church. But no more. The Eastern Orthodox Church still emphasizes Christ the Pantocrator, the solemn regal Jesus astride the world, coming in judgment. But more and more the Western church emphasizes the servant-shepherd-king, the self-emptying Jesus who reigns out of a deep self-giving mercy. There is truth in both images, but there is also comfort in the image emphasized in our time. In an age sorely burned by tyranny and power, in a time of ethnic cleansing and the holocaust of millions in brute cruelty, we need an image of One who holds power in wounded hands, in hands outstretched, with heart open to receive. And so the woman-in-love celebrates the real power of her Beloved — love's power to melt the hardest of hearts, and heal with tears.

This then becomes the backdrop for the final theme of Ordinary Time, the return of the Lover. It is the time of the Eschaton, the end-time. The readings are those of Jesus the judge, and the woman-in-love gathers her children to give an account. Advent celebrated his coming in *history*, in time past. The Church at prayer celebrates his coming in *mystery*, his presence now in and out of her awareness, his presence keeping her bound to him in faith. Now, at the end of Ordinary Time, the church faces the inevitable — his final return to claim his own. It is his coming in *majesty*, and only those wearing the strong fiber of the wedding garment will be able to endure his gaze. Those clothed in the rough weave of a life stitched with threads of loving, his gaze will make radiant. His gaze will become cauterizing to those unclad in their nakedness. For he was hungry and remained so. He thirsted, and was not given a drink; was naked and was not clothed. Those bereft of the loving that threads the pieces of our life together will burn with embarrassment in the face of a love that emptied itself out for their sakes. Indeed, they will want the hills to cover them so that they might hide.

The days are growing chill, the air crisp. The time of winter approaches, and the days grow shorter. Darkness comes early. As the church's year comes to a close, the woman-in-love prepares herself to begin once again, the great watch, the waiting time. The seasons of the soul have come full circle. Ever ancient, ever new, she will begin again, for her Lover is always the same; but a part of her is not the same in her earthy journey. She is what he has made her, his very body throughout time in the world, but as time unfolds she will become more and more who she really is, as once again she prepares to relive — the seasons of the soul.

Footprints

Virgin snow I do not know where to walk

or even if I should.

The Way?
You stand in it
and the prints
are underneath your shoes.

What is essential
is invisible to the eye.

The heart knows.

C.M. Streeter, O.P., 1983

Conclusion

The Christian Is a Person-in-Love

These reflections have attempted to form a setting for a jewel. The jewel is the Word, both in person, and in the Scriptures. A jewel can be viewed on the kitchen table. But a jewel will be much better viewed on black velvet under soft light. The setting is key to the viewing, for it forms the ambiance, the tone, the mood, for the seeing itself.

Christians of various denominations long for a personal relationship with Christ Jesus. They read the Scriptures, yet they sense something is missing. What might be missing is the setting for the jewel. One of the results of our disunity is the fact that, like squabbling children, we have each run off with a part of our Christian inheritance, clutching it close to our chests in our hot little hands. The Christian inheritance is not mine nor yours. It is *ours*. Liturgical and sacramental abuse was a major cause of the division of the Christian community. One way to begin to heal that division will be the restoration of a proper liturgical setting for the Word.

It has been the major thrust of this little work to create a wider and truer context for liturgical celebration, free from any narrow ritualism that could masquerade as the real thing in some worshiping communities of varying denominations. The only way I know to avoid this is to intentionally link ritual with the Incarnate Word as a continuance of his presence in the world in the community we call Church. With this deliberate link, rather than being a perfunctory set of rites, ritual can flex, it can grow, it can once again become living. Additionally, understanding the liturgical gathering of the community as an encounter with the Church's Beloved can contribute to safeguard it from any manipulation that risks betraying the words of the Gospel itself.

How will we as communities of faith get to this point? I suspect it will come with a simultaneous conversion of both leadership and congregational members. When the presider understands his or her role in this light, and the congregation is aware of its dignity, the entire congregational dough is leavened and will rise. Baked in the oven of faithful practice, this bread will not only nourish, it will draw those from the highways and byways by its fragrance.

Practically speaking, this will mean that both leaders and followers will have to fall in love. We are not used to speaking in such romantic terms about religion, yet it would serve us well to stop at the wayside shrine of the erotic to ground our devotion once again in a respect for the human. It is being pointed out to us that there is a powerful movement in all the cosmos toward communion. Erotic sexual activity makes it most explicit, but there are traces of this alluring energy all about us. When we discover the intense longing with which the Word took on our human limitation, we are amazed. If we allow ourselves to follow the course of this divine desire through the life of Jesus, we can become mute with wonder.

Falling in love romantically is something we would not give up for the world. Painful as it is, unnerving as it is, we never feel as alive as when we have fallen in love. Our body chemistry changes. We become euphoric, and can't turn it off. We do things we would never do if we were not in love. Our bones become rubber, we blush, we feel as though our soul has been pierced and our very selves are leaking out. We become weak in the knees, sweaty, embarrassed, and very vulnerable, and we wouldn't change all this for the world. Why? We are made to be people in love. We are the only species that can be aware of what it does to us. It borders on the ecstatic, and we long to be taken clean out of ourselves and carried off. We deliberately use drugs, alcohol, and sex to trigger this temporary ecstasy, and can get addicted to them because of their effects. We do it again and again to try to create a semi-permanent *state*. And here we can take our cue.

We are made from love. We have been created out of nothing but Love, in and through the communing love of two human beings. The Mystery behind all of this must be trying to tell us something. But an act of love is different from being in *a state* of love. Being in love as a state is a condition. It is a way of *being*. I jolly well know the difference of my state of being when I am in love and when I'm not. It is unmistakable.

To speak of myself as a person-in-love then is to refer to a condition I find myself in. I am experiencing myself in a certain way. Today I'm in love. Yesterday I wasn't. Today my values are different. I see life through my love. I'm changed. Perhaps this is what people are trying to describe when they say they "got religion." Something has changed. I'm different now.

As with romantic love, falling in love with God has its infatuation stage. I "get religion" and feel on cloud nine for a time, but honeymoons end, and then diapers need to be changed. So it is with religious experience. Infatuation with the experience itself must give way to genuine self-giving love of the person, or the relationship remains stuck in mutual self-gratification. So it is with religious love.

I need to listen to my Beloved. I need to show up. I need to spend time. In good times and bad I need to be there. I need to give and learn to receive. My love needs to learn to be discreet, at times open, at times shy. It needs to learn fairness, for justice is one of its first expressions. It needs to be courageous, moderate, brave, and balanced, both in facing my needs and the desires of my Beloved. My love needs to become stronger than death and harder than hell, and my Beloved will not stop until it has become so. This is what it means to be a person in the state of being-in-love religiously with the Divine, manifested in the Word. This is what needs to happen to both presider and individual Christian. We need to be persons-in-love.

It takes one to know one. The intimacy of a strong and true relationship with the Word is contagious. The Word has said he has come to cast fire upon the earth. Day following upon day, through the seasons of the soul, may we all become radiant with that conflagration.

I want to know...

Seedling,
what makes you grow?

I want to know.

Warmth of Sonning
or tears shed
by skies that miss the Son?

I want to know.

Fragile thing,
your mystery defies my probing —
Hold, my hand,
lest you disturb the secret
and by uprooting
kill the process
unfolding gently 'midst the fertile dark.

C.M. Streeter, O.P., 1982